WATER GUEST

WISCONSIN POETRY SERIES

Sean Bishop and Jesse Lee Kercheval, *series editors*
Ronald Wallace, *founding series editor*

WATER GUEST

Caroline M. Mar

THE UNIVERSITY OF WISCONSIN PRESS

Publication of this book has been made possible, in part, through support from the Brittingham Trust.

The University of Wisconsin Press
728 State Street, Suite 443
Madison, Wisconsin 53706
uwpress.wisc.edu

Printed in the United States of America

Library of Congress Cataloging-in-Publication Data
Names: Mar, Caroline M., 1983- author.
Title: Water guest / Caroline M. Mar.
Description: Madison, Wisconsin : University of Wisconsin Press, 2025. | Series: Wisconsin poetry series
Identifiers: LCCN 2024032672 | ISBN 9780299352646 (paperback)
Subjects: LCGFT: Poetry.
Classification: LCC PS3613.A68 W38 2025 | DDC 811/.6—dc23/eng/20240905
LC record available at https://lccn.loc.gov/2024032672

for my ancestors

. . . at last the Lake burst upon us—a noble sheet of blue water lifted six thousand three hundred feet above the level of the sea, and walled in by a rim of snow-clad mountain peaks that towered aloft full three thousand feet higher still!

. . . As it lay there with the shadows of the mountains brilliantly photographed upon its still surface I thought it must surely be the fairest picture the whole earth affords.

—MARK TWAIN describing Lake Tahoe, *Roughing It*

The precise number of Chinese who worked on the railroad from 1864 to 1869 is not clear; records are incomplete and inexact . . . Historians estimate that at any one time as many as 10,000 to 15,000 Chinese were working on constructing the railroad. Most Chinese probably did not work for the entire duration of construction and others would take their place, particularly because the work was so difficult and dangerous.

—STANFORD UNIVERSITY, Chinese Railroad Workers in
    North America Project

someone will remember us
            I say
        even in another time
—SAPPHO, Fragment 147
    trans. Anne Carson

Contents

WATER GUEST

遺 産

Where can I set this inheritance down?
Maybe every winter was like this, once.

     I know every winter was like this once,
     the whiteness devised to draw us in.

The ways whiteness devises to draw us in:
We will not hurt you. A gentle approach.

     It won't hurt you; take the gentlest approach:
     a rustic wood bench, a sheepskin throw pillow.

Rustic wood benches, sheepskin throw pillows;
who needs a fence when the bears walk through?

     No need for a fence. The bears walk through,
     always hungry. They do so much needing.

I am always hungry, full of my needing.
I know how to spend an inheritance down.

Failed Translations

after Poem #8, Angel Island

1.

Nation   not   cow   ,
                 beautiful   .
                 tall   green   ,
                              is   ?

2.

Country   not   why   why   oxen   ,
         out   beautiful   .
                 tall   un/ocean-green ,
                      maybe   is   blue   ?

3.

Country
              that is not mine
                              ox-tied,
gazing out
              gorgeous hillsides
                              and wanderers.
This tall ship sails me
                      sea-green
                              nearer,
wondering
              what it is
                         this rising blue?

Dream of the Lake

You are not the sea, but I confuse you
with the sea, awash in the blood
beneath my skin

> What are the sailor's tools
> What burns me to the touch

Slipknot
Bowline knot
> *Better to know a knot*

On your surface, my skin darkens
all summer, blood-brown
like a tree's rough bark

> My unanswered questions
> uprooted and sky-turned

Clove hitch
Sheet bend
> *and not need it*

Here: let me anchor you
I can't say blood blooms, as if
it wasn't the other way around

> I'm no fish,
> you're no ocean

Rolling hitch
Stopper knot
> *than to need a knot*

I see you looking at me, my blood
gutters, gathering
like baubles off a broken string

                    I an unspooled skein,
                    a daughter unmoored

        and not know it

Mythology

The partial truths: That the water preserves. That the water
    is so cold it slows bacterial action. What is false: That the water
keeps whole, that there are no fish to nibble the morsels
    of cheek and jowl, the curl of an eyelid. That the water is clear
to a depth of one hundred feet. In fact, it is clear to a depth
    of sixty-nine. At least, this was true at last measure, a disk in the water,
a wavering white eye seen until it sputters closed, though
    it depends upon weather, season, and algae content within the water.
That there are hundreds, held down deep, eyes open, seeking
    the shoreline's rocky light, empty sockets and insolent grins.
That there is a creature, maybe beastly, maybe beautiful,
    cruising her slow, sweet way through the watery canyons
of glacier-carved granite. That there is a tunnel connecting elsewhere,
    that this is what allows bodies drowned here to finally float up
in some other lake. That there are mysteries we cannot solve
    deep beneath this surface, in that darkness below seventy feet.
That we cannot know. That what we do not know,
    we imagine, we retell. That the water's whispers are worth retelling.

Stage 1: Cold Shock
Threat No. 1 Loss of Breathing Control

Gasping

There are an average of seven drownings per year in the lake, most due
to cold water shock, even among those who are capable swimmers. Or were
before the water folded them into itself:

a pocket of failure, a slipped

seam of darkness out of the summer

sun's light.

Hyperventilation

My body in the summer heat, skin a prickling of sweat, the stick
of flesh to seat before I rise, look out over the edge, and dive.

My lungs seizing together inside my chest: a cavity curling inward.
The body, built for survival. The water still icy from snowmelt.

Difficulty holding your breath

It takes a certain force to move your limbs
        as you tread water. Remember to cup your hands,
like this. To kick just so, and steady.
        To keep your neck above the waves, to gulp air
like guilt, to hold it before you let it go.

Feeling of suffocation

I have felt this shock in my own body. The delicate line
between body and brain. The pain
of doing the thing that keeps you alive.

Stage 1: Cold Shock

Threat No. 2 Heart and Blood Pressure Problems

Cold water immersion causes my body to shudder, to shock,
an instantaneous and massive exuberance and joy,
increase in heart rate and blood pressure because there is racing doubt, possibility of failure,
all the blood vessels in your skin might explode, or might survive, might
constrict in response to the body? A live wire, electric, dangerous, it is
sudden cooling, which is far more intense against the water's conductivity, deeper
in water than in air. In vulnerable cells, the cold awakens something,
individuals, this greatly increases my certainty that my life has meaning.
the danger of heart silly heart, hopeful heart, busted heart,
swim through
failure and stroke.

Stage 1: Cold Shock
Threat No. 3 Mental Problems

aquaphobia: fear of water, specifically of drowning
claustrophobia: fear of suffocation and restriction
hydrophobia: fear of water
    though the human body is 80 percent water
ichthyophobia: fear of fish
    that time we ate lobster on a beach in Cuba and you laughed and laughed, delighted
    that your fear had subsided, you no longer believed
    it was swimming around inside you
xenophobia: fear of the unknown
chromophobia: fear of a color
    in this case, I suppose the color
    would be blue
achluophobia, or *nyctophobia*, or *scotophobia*, or *lygophobia*: fear of darkness
    most children have this, it is not abnormal
    to fear the loss of a sense, sight being
    one upon which we rely heavily to understand what is happening
    around us, just look
    how many names, though none
    are clinical
thanatophobia: fear of dying
phobophobia: fear of fear
    : fear of not being found
        those rumors, again—
        all those bodies
    : fear of being found
    : fear of being too late

With a surface area of 191.6 square miles and a depth of 1,645 feet, Lake Tahoe is the largest and the second-deepest alpine lake in the United States

Emma says the lake is the most beautiful place in the country.
    Darren says *Fuck yeah*.
        The water

    is all pleasure, slipped skin and sunrise, cerulean skyshine
        like a piece of just-cracked sea glass.

                    Darren says
these are some of the best mountains anywhere, which is saying a lot
    because he dropped out of school in Colorado for the mountains.

        Cold
    even at its Caribbean blue edges, wind-rushed

          and lung-flushed with every dive, the water
      envelops and whispers, whispers:

              I'm dangerous.

    The body
        of a diver was finally recovered, seventeen years later.

Emma says she means it, says she first thought it years ago
    when she biked across the country. Melissa says maybe

we just take it for granted, all this beauty, because we see it so often.
        An edge reflects

under all that beauteous bauble, the shimmer and slick
        of a summer swim.

                        Emma's parents, then Emma's sister,
                                got married here, at the lake.

The body was locked below a ledge, unable to float, to surface.

Imagine drowning   in a scuba mask.

Sandy says *This doesn't suck* every time we ride out
        on the water, or Melissa does.   Someone always says it.

What I think about:
                the body below the shelf, preserved.
                Seventeen years. That's how cold
                the water is.

                        In the darkest depths, the cold
                        must become unbearable, all skin-crush and sink,
                        crisp snap, pressure to bone.

                What a startle
                        he must have been,
                for the now-divers, the live divers.
                        Like a ghost, an alien, a terrible

                        mirror: here you are, reflected
                                in the water's depths.

Mostly, it's the mountains that are reflected. Lately
        there's been lots of haze—the forest fires. It's hard to remember
                the drought, Mark says,
    when there's all this water around.

                The diver in repose.

He must have looked like he was resting, eventually,

            struggle gone out.

                        Do you tear it out, fight
                                the water, or simply keep sucking
                    at absence.

The water is not all pleasure, though it promises
                        sweetness, sure delight.

The water, clean
            and clear, made
                            for both worlds:
                            to float
                            to drown.

Naming

Blank sky: too simple. You are window-streaked, edged in god's-eye-white. I can see
where you took a breath, where you repeated yourself. Tiny flecks of your own voice,
    deepening.
Clear as an eye drop. Settled as a vintage tear. Nothing harried about you, tiny fingers
    licking
your own edges. You could be a flag, flutter in anticipation of your own Wellfleet
    wedding.
Something old, something borrowed, a rusty earring back cast aside. You are summer's
generosity, watermelon's thinnest rind, your firework tongue in my shell-shine mouth.
The antique ocean blooms, watches.

Intelligible

My name a rearing horse, curved into
its evolution. Logographic,

four legs like drops of sweat falling
from a shaking body.

The etymological—or is it orthographical—
origin of the word *clear* is the word *blue-green*.

Radical : water : drops from a brush
on a page, swishing into newness, so

becoming : the clarity we use for death.
Semantic-phonetic, each stroke's symbiosis

of sound and meaning. A morpheme
rather than a phoneme. Clear morning,

we greet our dead and deathly, send gifts
for the moving-on. Not darkness, nor night :

our dead aren't afraid of the day's blue face.
May our dead float back to this thin surface, deep

blue to blue-green to clear. I see the way the light
moves through the water. The way the light moves

through. What is it you do to honor your dead
in the after? In an account I read, you burn them,

too. We all need something to carry
into the next world. Its watery edge. I know

what I said : I don't believe in any next thing.
Yet I see ghosts, see memory. Look how I am

haunted. The smoke like a clot in my lung.
Shh, shh, drink now. The water is cool.

Rinse the ash from your face.

Burials

Unrest affects the living.   Melba tells me
story after story: there once was a Chinatown

in Dayton, Nevada. It ended   like so much else
in this wild and wilder   West. Bodies, a pit, a thundering

of hooves. Later, a motel,   and when a cabinet was built
into the basement: skulls stacked like rocks

behind foundation walls.   Grinning ghosts,
awaiting their shining   moment.

We believe there's danger in living on top of burials.
Later, a woman living   there committed suicide.

Like every Chinatown   the motel burned down.
The ghosts won out, their own   incensed offering.

Elsewhere, the power   company dug in to set
a line and found   instead, a body—

Sent off: forensics: determination: *Washoe*.
They shipped him   to her at the museum.

But I just thought—   *I had this feeling—*
She looked it up, what   we do when we do it

our way. Buried him   with red silk, oranges,
faced him   to the East.

Stage 2: Physical Incapacitation

When the waters rose, the forest stayed. What else can a forest do
but stand. There would be no fire inside the lake.

There would be no ground to tumble down. Just water rising,
cold and blue, the floods of the next era.

Sometimes the change comes over you like that all at once. A drowning.

Hundreds of coolies were tied together and weighed down
with rocks. Straw hats removed, queues tangled, thrown in to save

the cost of their pay. The historians say this is unlikely. Given
the railroad payrolls showing each Chinese contractor paid,

given how little Chinese labor cost, given the distance
from the Truckee railroad camp to the lake. Given

every other history I know:
chains, bodies of water, ghosts—

Sometimes a person isn't a person at all, but a weight
to be freighted onto someone else's shoulder.

Why not the silent lake? Why not a flood of furious bodies
fighting toward the coldest surface?

The forest stayed, and drowned.

Portraits of the Ancestor

a twisting torso, feet in third position, your body's ballet the way
you throw the dirt from the shovel's tip, gunpowder bloom
darkening the sky.　　　　the rest of you so still
in the camera's click-step.
the *swish* of the dirt leaving the shovel, your symphony.

*

pulling a handcart, signature
coolie hat on each of your heads, but you
I recognize by the bowing of your legs.
maybe this is why my thigh bones curve
away from each other
the way your shoulders spread
to pull each arm of the handcart, wheels clunking
over chunky rock, dust, over gravel.
the heat is so much that you need long sleeves.
to shield you. I need sun on my skin to know
I belong to you, yours.

*

a turned back, a stooped shoulder.

1870 census; Truckee, CA:
Ah John, male, 18; occupation: prostitute

In some other lover's story, I'd die
in this lake for you, lover. Or I'd lie
undisturbed in sleep, you'd have no other.
The passion of the cut sleeve: the lover
too precious to mess with, no walkabout,
roundabout, look-see loves, fucking about
any way you want to, lover. Fuck all
your old mothers, dead in ground, maggoty.
My name on your tongue the wrong one to call.
Somebody tell me why the word faggotry
feels so fucking good in the mouth. They see
one who certainly had a braid silk-strewn,
elements of a dandy in him. Me?
I'll die in this lake, and you'll die too soon.

Stage 3: Hypothermia

The lake is steel-shirred gray, a sheet of velvet,
soft-napped. Water barely stirring. The snow
is loud as an earthquake, house shaking

with dropped weight as the slide overcomes
the roofline. Winter's thundering reminder:
some things cannot be stopped.

The snow is loud beneath the plow, its spray
an arc of meditation. The snow clings, a sticky sheet,
to the sides of the sweating trees. This cannot last

forever. Snow melts into the lake, the icy rocks.
Winter: gray and gray and gray; crystalline
whiteness. The gray-dark water will not freeze,

the lake too deep. And what can survive
that kind of cold? *Nothing, nothing*, my mind's
lie: the fish are fattening, swimming slow.

Yes, too, the snow is quiet. Muffling every sound
but the crunch of my footfalls following
the shape of your boot prints, as I follow you.

S---- Valley

the trail winds down the mountain's side, tree line
hiding what might kill you:

ice crevice, creek not quite gone cold
enough to freeze, or another tree, solid

as a wall you can smash a body against. you knew a boy
who smashed like that, popped

his collarbone clean in two, helicoptered home. another
crushed his truck into a tree, wheel-bent and beer-

bottled as he tumbled onto asphalt: still living.
what kind of boy was it, you wonder, who climbed

this gorgeous ridge and thought: I ought to name
this valley. I ought to name whatever comes

into my line of sight, call it after a woman like I call
everything I've ever owned *she* and *her*.

a boy in uniform, a boy who didn't think
of what might already have been named.

when you were young, you loved a boy
who put his fist into a wall. you understood

boys might someday want to put their fists
into your body. breakable: what they were raised

to be. comfort them, comfort them. be the woman
who can tend their busted-down beds

of need. a woman teaching them how to be better.
what to tender, what not to break.

oh, what an old and boring story.
you'll have to dig, to ask around, but you'll find it:

this valley's name might be memdéwi ʔitMúʔuš.
might be no-one-remembers-for-sure. you know

how to learn what you can. you knew to run off like a deer,
be a body of your own riding down

the ridge, not raising the next line
of boys. not when some other mother's boy

might stride across some mountain,
look you in your face, call you a name you know

is not what you are called.

Fire Control

In the forest I love, they spent one hundred years
suppressing every urge to burn. We always make
the same mistakes: stem each tide, smother every spark.
These drought years or the damp before, it didn't matter—

fire stopped at every cost, though nature wants
to be burned to bone every now and again.
The pines remember to burst themselves
open. This is one way to grow.

In the campfire, the flame's blue-hot center
is the color of the lake. The same wavering shape, a tear
sliding down the cheek of some childhood drawing.
A gold miner's pickax, or a railroad laborer's,

would be made mostly of iron, though the handle of course
would be wood. Smooth-worn by hardened hands.
An ache of smash and shatter. Once, in this forest I love,
Samuel Clemens came and made a timber claim.

Another way to strike it rich. One night he turned
to gaze upon the lake, and his supper set
this forest we loved blazing. Love meaning
different things to each of us, I'm sure.

The melting point of gold is one thousand nine hundred
forty-eight degrees Fahrenheit. The average wildfire
has a temperature of one thousand four hundred
seventy-two degrees, and can reach two thousand

one hundred ninety-two at the fire front.
Fire burns every kind of money.
I wonder why they call the flame a tongue, the searing lick
of pain. I think of all our metaphors for love:

from burning.
Yes, the fire could burn through everything
you'd have wanted to touch. One accident
defined the year of my birth, the rest of my father's life.

A fire can make us see the past differently.
Our family name is painted on the side
of the Harley's gas tank. His brother's name
is the growl of the gasoline's combustion.

One hundred years of avoiding that burn, now
bark beetles shuck the trees to hollow shells.
One hundred twenty-nine million trees are dead
in the Sierra Nevada. Untamable range, tamed by swing

of axe and hammer. Dynamite.
On a fire day, I stare at the sky's yellow pallor. In the Sierra's
ochre foothills, even the flower heads wither
in the windy heat. The tree growth is so dense the fire moves

like a string of fevered kisses after the drought
of a long separation. Humans are responsible
for 84 percent of forest fires.
In a prescribed burn, only enough trees are taken to stem

the beetle's tide, to give earth some room to breathe.
Healthy competition for the smallest sprouts.
Each June, pollen coats our steps like a blanket of gold.
On a fire day, I sweep instead the tawny grit of soot,

of swishing charcoal streaks. The melting point of iron
is twenty-eight hundred degrees. Maybe this
is all that survives. In any forest, there's only room
for so many. The *Truckee Method*: when the fourth fire

fails, starve them out. Turn in whiteness
against the *unmitigated curse* and boycott
any contact with us. Slow burn of strangulation.
The western bark beetle is the size of a grain

of rice in the bowl of a *coolie slave*. It is not
an invasive species, knows these dry and dense conditions.
Sometimes the fire starts within, and the melting point
is a door slamming shut. The western bark beetle

doesn't care about the coming fire until, I suppose,
it is trapped inside it. On a fire day, I can't help but imagine
this horror. The beloved body, a sacrifice
to the fire's demands.

One hundred twenty-nine million dead trees
waiting for the fire's burn. Humans are probably responsible
for each of these repeated mistakes.
Mark Twain became Mark Twain because he burned

the forest's easy money. The *Truckee Method* was touted
as a great success. My father refuses to live in a house
with an automatic garage door, but every day rides out
on the bike that sent the spark. On a fire day,

children are not allowed outside without masks.
Unmitigated curse might be the Earth's secret name
for humanity. The melting point of steel
is twenty-five hundred degrees. Bone does not melt

but burns. What is the melting point of history?
On a fire day, I stand on our front steps, watch
another crimson sunrise. The flames swallow air
and the water swells with ash.

Stage 4: Circum-rescue Collapse

an erasure

can happen just before   The symptom

     faint   . But, why

                      fight   to stay alive,

                                 survive. Once

       a mental relaxation

       can drop   can fail

                             remember   heart   is

                                 the water. Knowing

     a   difference.

     it is this

   the greatest   survival. Some of these actions might even seem counter-

intuitive   ,   you understand

.

Catalog of Writings Left by
Chinese Railroad Laborers of the C.P.R.R.

[   ]
[   ]
[   ]
[   ]
[   ]
[   ]
[   ]
[   ]
[   ]
[   ]
[   ]
[   ]
[   ]
[   ]
[   ]
[   ]

水 客

the water a guest inside of us
salty-sweet and swimming
how water does and you
a guest in your own house
a watery word
a guest on the tongue
a gust of air across wet lips   a voice
echoing back and back
though nothing's left to prove it no
papers no shred of evidence not one
letter not one mark upon the page
no papers
no papers
your papers
for a period of three long years
an ocean away from where you are not
a guest   where are you from
people ask me   ask people who look
like me   look like anything but
the blankness of a page
let me turn then to the color
of water into ink ground against a stone
the words carried back by each water guest
each bringer of news and love and tribulation here
are the words that belong to you
here are the words that belong

高祖父：　A Correspondence　　　：太爺

I have no one left to ask, here
so I write to ask you these things.

Did you ever see this lake? Were you one
of those who scaled that nearby pass?
As you looked across this gorgeous landscape, all
granite all tallpine all blueair, tell me
what you thought—

I am certain you could write, would write,
would have written. And so someone read your letters
to your blinded son, and so he would recite later
all that he had learned because blindness
doesn't bind memory.

Did you mistake the moraine's slide, glacier-carved
like the face of your forgotten daughters,
for struggle?

Did you hate the mountains for the work—
armswing pickswing hammerswing shovelswing—
they wrung out of you?

Though I am not certain you could write,
would write, would have written, maybe
you did. That someone would have read
your letters to your barely literate son, that
he might know your voice in his ear.

When you were here, did the woods still smell
of baked rock, crumbled sugar pine? Or had the silt
and gilt timber barons already tumbled it all down
to the water's murk-washed edge?

清 明: we burn you paper gifts, incense, oranges
in a pile. Flowers and flowers upon each grave.

The ghosts of those who died in these mountains
are doomed forever. The One-eyed Wanderer,

exploded to just a hand. Old Three-moles, washed
away in a dam burst. Squeakylaugh impaled on a rail.

Longteeth. Shitforbrains. Short Chung and Fat Chung,
both. No body means nobody to bury, no body

to call home. No one to tell them
hit the road, cross over, cross over—

Would it be so bad if these mountains were your
eternity? The thinner air of heaven.

The mountains are calling and I must go.

The blue like a lance to your heart.

Blue the basin the basket the berry the juice blue that counters the yellow of bleach bluing
blue indigo blue dye #4 blue the bruise the bitter blue anything but an eye please blue
the water the wash the vein in my body the vein in my earth our earth the sapphire
blue the glittering dark sky at night sky at day sky at blue note sounding blue the print
the plan the next step into blue the brazen the bold the navy the few the proud who
wants that blues sing it again sister bluer than blue my blue blood true blood tv fantasy
blue light blue screen blue movie blue balls blue butch blue black battered and beaten
or blue like a piece of glass with the sun shining through it blue as a shard a shatter a
splatter of water blue blur that won't leave me don't sparkle for just anything don't break

My father loves to tell your departure:
how you crashed from the open window into the garden
to escape your brother's swinging sword, how this was what drove you
to ship, to sea, to foreign shore.

How in your body's absence,
your brother blinded your baby for spite.
Your eyes turned toward the track's next turn.

Heaven could be the smell of pines
and snowmelt under your boots.

Heaven could be the color of this water
at precisely twenty-two feet deep.

My father wrote his father's story, how first your brother
and later he, your eldest son, departed to cover
your foolish debts. Your rescue from debtor's prison.
But there was, too, a before, though your son never told him
what it was like when you yourself were away
making some kind of living in 金山.

What I don't know:

The blast of dynamite.
The whistle of engine.

Dreams of railroad spikes falling
from your son's eyes.

Am I mistaken, calling this place *beauty*. Nothing
but leisure-seeking on the lake's cool skin.
Unperturbed, the water slips into
my mouth whenever I swim.

who tutored your son to memorize the texts
he must have later used to teach his students
what was done to his mother in your absence
if she was your only wife, her name, the names
of your son's wives who were not my great-
grandmother, the names of his non-surviving
children who were my great-aunts and -uncles,
whether he was gentle or harsh with them,
the names of your non-surviving children, of any
of the servants, who it was you loved, if anyone,
if you wanted to kill your brother, too, and why
you didn't, what it was like when you returned

what happened to your brother when he returned,
what happened to you in debtor's prison, what was done
to your wife in your absence, or the two before her,
their names, the names of your non-surviving children
一 and 二, the names of her sisters, her mother, her
friends, whether you were gentle or harsh, if it was you
who taught my grandfather not to use his hands
on children, who it was you loved, if anyone, if you wanted
to stay or to leave, what it was like when you returned

I understand why you don't answer.

I know the answers. There are
no answers. I am the only
possible outcome here.

Let's not pretend you would have cared
what happened to me except I am
your dream of 金山 made real—

My rings: of gold. My dress: of gold.
My eyes: of gold. My skin: of gold.
My mouth: my mouth: my mouth.

Of late—no, since I was a child—
I've spent a lot of time wondering
about the *bachelor society*.

What secrecy that invites: all those bodies,
men and male, kept close
in their togetherness.

I read only silence.

Did a 水客 carry your letters for you? I, too,
would be a guest in your house, a guest
made of water, a guest in every house
on this land that shouldn't belong to me.

Golden goddess of good luck, god
of glory and gory success, shine of someone's
fortune, scent of dragon scale and slippery
glinting teeth: you chase and chase it.

What song survives
the work you did, the stories you told

your blind son waiting for your return

                                        your mute son waiting for your return

        your daughters lost to history like your letters

When you died did you hear
music? Was it the clinking tone
of iron into fresh-laid track?

I can make you whoever
I need you to be, but I can't stop
asking you these questions.

Tell me, how did you die?

                        It was you who died in the street:
                        your old head unbent and unbowed
                        before a soldier's rifle butt.

What is your relationship
to color? Does 藍 even begin
to cover it? Is 金 a color?
I know no nuance in this
un-simplified tongue.

水, 金: two words I still remember.

When I say 茶, your
great-   granddaughter
mocks my singing accent, lilt
of my gold-laden tongue
against your language's watery shore.

Tiger balm smell of 嫲 嫲's sore knees.
I imagine your knees after each day's labor.
Your shoulders' ache. Each body's work takes
a different weight. Who was the one who rubbed
the knots, who laid a sweet and gentle palm—
though rough, like yours—
against your tender hurts?

Tell me about him, who
loved you best. Who you hid,
who hid you.

your lips   Was it   your lips,
                                   to
                                   pressed in those claustrophobic
                                   kindling rooms?

In Hong Kong, I was shy to speak
to the other women. *I have a girlfriend,
too*, finally, then laughter. A culture
of women away from family and homeland,
awash in women's work and the ways
it buckled them, but still: a kind of relief.

You're teaching me the beauty
of revisionist history. I make you lovers
because, yes, it is in my power, because
my ancestral altar needs a queerer root.
Because, too, I am afraid of the smoke-
thick danger of you if you were not:

girl children in locked cages—

who could love a man like that?

How quick the language slips
from our gold-plated tongues.

I have been keeping secrets
from the woman I love.

Here's what I remember:
我愛你。紅。海。
東南西北。

I remember my name, part
of my father's and his father's.
I never knew

yours.   yours.

I should have asked your granddaughter
when I had the chance. I should have
known your name.

                                        I should have asked your son
                                    when I had the chance. I should have
                                                  known your name.

Tell me about your mistakes,
what they cost you. Blood
on your palm, or tears in your mouth.
So like sweat on the tongue.

I am sure this was not your dream.

I was not your dream.

The kindling rooms: every plank a match unstruck,
a burn waiting to consume. Every Chinatown
burned down more than once.

Picturing you driven out: a stick against
your strong back, a frothing white face
spitting rage race and fear. Or maybe
you were one of those who went out,
bought a rifle or two, armed in the way
of your temporary homeland.

I'm not sure our hands aren't bloody.
I am losing track of each detail
I have forgotten, like the wood inlay
chipping slowly out of my 箱.

Maybe it's your blood I feel tingling
when I turn my own gun in my palm.
We know what it is to defend ourselves.

I like the smell of my own skin
after sun, and the smell of pine
pitch, and pollen. Is this vanity?

This story may have gotten away from us.
Your life unravels

off my unruly hand.

I do not understand why you don't answer.

I think I am telling the wrong story. I think
I care more about your wife, your wives, your
long-dead daughters.

When you raise a daughter,
you are raising someone else's slave.

Don't they still belong to me?

I could decide to make you happy.

Gold is the eye the tongue the lion
Gold the mountain the valley the river gold
the nugget the ingot the flake the flume
the fairy the dust the feather the fatherland
Gold the sun and the sunlight the son
You wanted sons and sons and sons
Gold the daughter in spite of gold
the bangles and bracelets and rings
Gold the ornate and elaborate
Hold me, here: this is my ordinary hand

Because *only barbarians touch like that*

I am free to build you in my own image.

Your mouth on another man's mouth
unafraid or maybe afraid, quiet
in a boardinghouse bed or a canvas tent
the hurried rush of your bodies
before shift change or exhaustion or
the call to supper. The joy of it.

I'd rather not be gold-dusted, shimmer
of bronzers and glimmering lotions, potions
of nanoparticles that never break down
and will float forever in this water, in the gut
of a fish, in my blood. No.

I'd rather think about blue.

The waves tick the clock of my patience.
Each pine a pictogram of response:
here, a word on your gratitude; here,
a word on your hunger.
I turn and turn the page but no more story comes.
You were here, I think,

perhaps stood where I stood.

You believed in shamans, oracles,
fortune tellers, other small gods.
What they told you about this future:

could you see me on this shore? A rock
in my palm, the shape
of an opened mouth.

You died   You died

seven thousand miles away.
The water is different water.
The trees are different trees.

How long the journey. How long
your death-blunted life. How long until I knew
even enough of our story
to know it wasn't enough.

I'm waiting for your echo to call back
across the smallest waves.

Swim, swim for the caves with me, let's find
the rock where our voices come singing.
Tell me how you survived winter.

Tell me about blue, about how you shouted
and shuddered when your feet touched the water
each time you bathed in the cold spring air.

三

Tragedy

One of the Chinese had been skewered by an iron brake rod and was
screaming for somebody to shoot him.
    —E. B. SCOTT, *The Saga of Lake Tahoe*

I think of the white man who lived after an iron rod—
also from the railroad, also a brake rod, perhaps—
speared him right through his brain. Medical marvel. The
conflicting accounts of whether or not the injury caused
personality change. Early neurology, psychology: his
daguerreotype affixed in the gilt-framed textbooks of our
memory. It is unclear whether [the Chinese] was, or was
not, shot. Whether he survived, was too a marvel with a
hole in his gut, or was it—no, had to be gut. To skewer
is to be food, gutted. The screaming implies not lungs,
nor throat. And the heart, well: death already. I have
screamed for somebody to let me die, but no one had
a gun. I was asking not to be saved. Oh, girlchild
sadness, epigenetic thread, disappointment stitched to
every story. In a different book, I read that [the Chinese]
had gunpowder hundreds of years before we put it to
guns. The Maya with wheels: the author's comparison.
When a tool's not worth the change it wrings. All
fireworks, no grenades; firecrackers without the cracking
of bullet. Just crush of knuckle to bone, iron to rib.
What interested the teller in this story was not the story's
inevitable end: a body, dead one way or another. Bones
shipped home for burial. A pallet box, or my father
coming home through customs: What you got in that
suitcase, son? My grandmother, he chuckles with each
retelling. We visit her every year, one of six names on a
stone. The index, too, lists six mentions of [the Chinese]
in 468 pages. *Caroline* is the name of a boat, one of 162

indexed. Home is where your living will honor you, as long as they remember you: a mean old woman. A skewering tongue in my father's childhood: bitterness. Either way, I know the man in the story is dead. Crawl of infection, loss of blood, shouting recoil of mercy: somebody's. It's been too long for a miracle. The water is meant for the rush of the hull. It doesn't count each dive. 144 years, waiting for someone to call his name.

Mercy

the phone wedged in my mouth like a seizure-stopper
flashlight spot-shined at the squirrel on the ground as I need

both hands to do the work both hands to grip the shovel about
which my friend said *maybe you'll laugh* after my desperate call

or maybe you won't and my father did chuckle a little with discomfort
or with letting me in on some secret of masculinity some rite

I wasn't supposed to get *I'm sorry*
there is no other way to end the life of a breathing thing

but a good strong arm in the end so the phone keeps my throat
from screaming while the dog whose fault all this is of course looks on

in what I think would be shame if shame were a thing
she could feel wagging her tail with a mix of fear and pride

for her near-kill and wondering though I don't think dogs can
wonder but if she can she is wondering why I am so unhappy

with her as I clench my teeth around the flashlight-
phone and I clench my fingers around the handle

of the shovel and I clench the small furred thing
that is my human-animal heart because I've always

been too tender to the touch
of suffering as it rolls and quakes each body

this body's furred tail curled like a rich woman's stole
and though everyone told me just one clean hit nothing in life

is clean so it takes three my teeth gritting *pleasepleaseplease*
against whatever I am breaking against the bricks

and the squeaking of the dog's need behind me
on the grass poor anxious thing with no sense

beyond herself what a way to live and I finish it
hard and set the shovel down with what dignity

I can muster and I say *I'm sorry I'm so sorry* after pulling
my spit-flecked phone from my mouth wiping it on my pajamas

and sliding back into the house and no that's not how
it ended it ended later as I shook and sobbed

on the bed the unstoppable wailing of a child who has been gravely
misunderstood or a woman who has lost

her sense of herself while the dog sat confused
in her delight at this my very worst thing though eventually

the night did end. and the sun rose next day and the pain grew
smaller with time almost the way the dog forgets near immediately

when I step on her tail yelping but then wiggling
with love when I tell her *I'm sorry I'm sorry so sorry*

長 衫

Mamah had this gaudy one: silk
the color of this water's shallowest edges
meant to be sky

& on that sky flew two gold bodies
dragon, phoenix: each finely stitched
in golden thread or thread

made gold-like by the weaving
of some kind of shimmering filament
a complicated overlap

of red and orange
of stitch and sparkle
& it did shine

The sun spiked itself out at the center
between those undulating beasts
fire-breathing and fire-born

& by center I mean I remember
the sun sat somewhere above
my navel when I put the dress on

when I spun in my certainty
I would grow up
& be beautiful: beautiful

Lay on the shine, coat me
like some dress that shows
exactly how much

the cost & look
I've become this
for you

Guest: First Translation

do I know your shape

writing in this, my language:

my not-language: the not-knowing

the looking up: what is the sign, again

dictionary, internet, verify: my memory

my guide

words I have never known

and then the sound:

for this, even Google has no answers.

Because our language is and is not a written language.

Because the computer's voice marbling shuǐké

in a dipping double fall-to-rise isn't speaking

our language but its bigger, steadier, colonizer cousin.

our language less shush and more bark

                    our language breaks more rules

I know shuǐ is really seoi2, know the Valley Girl lilt

of *tone two mid rising* in my mouth like I know

I would have written it *sui* for my mother to read aloud

as I practiced my writing tests

                              how it sounded in my pencil

                         swishing water's shape onto the page

but I have no sound for ké

could be 摔   like a hammer falling

or cyun1   like a village alone

or 街 gaai1   like a street with light shifting through it

Swim Team Outer Space

Katherine Bradford, 2020

Drowning moon, fulsome moon, moon
of gendered-baby pinks and blues, blood
moon, orb moon static in the paint-black sky:

how she hangs, how she suspends
the attentions of the swimmers below, the stars
that could, if closer, dwarf the light she reflects
in each cavern, each crevasse, pock-faced
rabbit moon, how I want to be one
of those swimmers, to swim in her light,
to breaststroke, confident, her dusty seas.

Song for Great-Grandfather

Your son's spindly fingers are mine, made me good at piano, means my fingers are yours, maybe the forehead, too, though I didn't get the ears, blooming like cliff woodbeauties. Lucky girl. My fingers can reach beyond a full octave. Keys merganser-dark, gull-white. Lanky, a pickax in your hand, the arm's sinuous extension, a flow like the water you must have known how to swim in. Your body turning, smooth, as we float in the water. The water is clear-cold, as always. It hurts when I open my eyes in the sunlight. A few brown trees among the green, the rocks dark-wet underwater like the backs of whales. Above the waterline, the sun glitters off the mica in the granite. Glitters off the water like day-stars. Still, I see you: your arm-swing sliding up and down the scale of the rocks

calls me forth, earthbound
each solid ring a note
someday, somewhere: song

Tie

the track is two bodies, never allowed to touch
the track is the maiden and the cowherd
the track is the stars on a clear night
the track is a clamor of hammers falling
the track is braces in your mouth, but heavier
the track is your own teeth, chattering
the track is warm to the touch
the track is waiting for the switch to pull
the track is lost somewhere in between
the track is slowly leached chemicals into earth
the track is bone-weary and has to lie down
the track is saying your name
the track is a thousand flattened pennies
the track is blood, on itself
the track is not a race, but a race
the track is miles and miles of open desert
the track is blinding sun on snow
the track is *their faces pealed and seared*
the track is looking at the sky, or it isn't
the track doesn't look at anything
the track is a mirror, distorted
the track is disoriented by directionality
the track is a binary
the track is a bindery
the track is a book: each tie a chapter
the track is a page
the track is a note, or a song, or an aria
the track is a metaphor, but you don't know for what
the track is an end unto itself
the track isn't going anywhere

Guest: Second Translation

Months later I will ride down the wide boulevards   of my city
with two strangers and a driver   the age of my father   same receding black hair

but lacking the milk-tall stance   and orthodontia smile
of the American-born, thus   reminding me more   of the generation before.

The strangers don't speak,   staring
at their phones   (as is the custom).   I stare

at his name, turning its tone   in my closed mouth.   It could be
Chi4 or even Chi3 but who would name   their child 廁

really.   I won't speak   until the strangers both leave the car,
mouth careful: *my father grew up in Chinatown* and   *how long*

have you lived here, Chi1?   deciding to go for tone one
like an optimistic song on my tongue   and he asks me

do I speak   廣東話   and I say 冇咁多
and he says he thinks it's better living   in the Richmond

than crowded Chinatown   and yes the Richmond is a lot like   the Sunset
where I grew up which is when it occurs

maybe he can answer   so at the next red light   I pull up
       my ghost-words   and say I know   水 but I don't know

this second one: can you help me   and he says oh yes:
his silver-edged bridge flashing   delight at the shore of his lip:

that's seoi2 haak3.

Means someone who travels back   and forth, like
a merchant or   an importer-exporter,   says it a few times

for me to practice   in my wobbly   克 - 黑 - 嚇 accent
       until I get it right: 客.

I say it used to mean   the people who carried
your letters home when no one   could leave   or come here

and he says   sure   it's still a lot like that
       they still use it   for those who go back

and forth   between here and there

           carrying what anyone needs.

Property

He said I was a baby because I cried over the loss of my property.

> —LUM MAY, merchant, recounting his encounter with Tacoma Mayor
> Weisbach after that same mayor led a mob to burn down what remained
> of Tacoma's Chinatown in 1885

What white man hasn't cried about what
he thinks belongs to him. I have seen them cry

and put fists through walls for the loss
of a car, or for being told

to sit back down, please, in their assigned seat.
I learned to fear men by hearing the stories

about how they would cry after they hit you,
say *forgiveness*, and make it your fault.

White men love to cry, for how hard
they miss the good old days, their fathers'

unsolvable love. Cry into their beers,
their whiskeys. See also:

an Irish wake. Even my grandfather,
I saw him cry, once, recounting the way

other men cried for their mothers
as the ship went down.

I am not a heartless bitch. I, too, am crying
writing white-teared words onto blue-white page.

But property, oh property,
what does a white man love

more than his manicured house.
Another powerful man crying, enraged

at his name being dragged through mud
that he made of spittle and beer. What tears

(I couldn't watch) made of the lies we tell
the secret selves we baby and coddle,

refusing to let them grow up. America,
you love the pornography of other people's

pain. Floods, fires, bullets: you think, in the end,
they probably got what was coming to them.

With a dry and pitying eye.
White men tell the most lies.

If my grandfather knew we would sell
the house after he died, he would have cried,

surely. Each leaf of ivy-climb carefully tended,
carefully loved. Each book in its rightful place.

My beloved not-rightfully country,
what are you but one long cry

of a white man claiming *mine*.
The cry of a man, soft hands

played too rough, coming
inside you, relieved-terrified at what it is

he's just done. Baby,
poor baby.

John Chinaman

runs the convenience store, the market, the laundry
is a money-launderer for the mob
plays the tables each Saturday night
plays the dozens
plays your mama and your mama and your mama with his soft lips
says your mama taste just as good as she looks
watches the door just in case
fought the law and the law won
has a scar on his eyelid to prove it
wishes his son could get into Harvard
hates affirmative action and all these lazy children
wears a jade pinky ring that he taps on his ivory cane
doesn't give a fuck that ivory is problematic
has a gold tooth, or four, or fourteen
has no teeth at all, but still laughter
married a nice girl from the village
married that too-good bitch from the city
worked his hands to the bone, you ungrateful
does not know why these ABCs got so much to complain about
isn't worried about it
sends money home every two weeks
still owes 40K to his smuggler
was a bricklayer, blacksmith, & baker
was a fisherman's son
was a cobbler's
was starving, or near it
knows his way around hunger
knows his way around a cleaver
knows his way around a needle
knows his way around a mouth
committed suicide, murder, or both

does what he has to do, dammit
has never gone hungry
thanks the ancestors, when he remembers
thanks his woman, rarely
thinks gratitude is for somebody weaker
thanks the work of these, his two hands

Celestials

Imperial dragon rolls his ball across the heavens

naughty monkey after everything   These stories

must have been the same when you were young

undulating across the sky: smoke tail, fire feather

the slip of juice from glut of eternal peaches

Imagine a golden scale, the weight of each claw:

cut glass tapping against the floors of heaven while gold drips

from melting lips and whiskers of filament

The phoenix has gone up again in plumes oh plumage

I would dress myself in your radiance for all my days

until I burned so much I had to plunge back into the lake

blue with heaven's reflection

Guest: Third Translation

that the guest is the only objective observer
who is a guest in my mouth
who will visit me when I am gone
(no one, no one)
whose customs can I call my own, can I crawl through
to traverse the other side
I have lost my objectivity, lost my object
of admiration, let me speak to
your manager, the customer is always
paying passage, passenger, a passing attempt
at an old goal, old ghost, older growth
I am lost in the forest for the trees
I am lost in the lake for the water, O,
there it is, then, the water:
I am arriving, I am arrived

Certainty

you know cliff diving to be dangerous and yet here you are granite beneath your feet ready
for anything if you could be ready as you can be in this life you're never really ready you
think you've heard you've called for a hovering leap a bound above the water so clear you
can see the bottom so clear and wouldn't you like that kind of clarity about everything is
this what it is that calls you to this water it is both clear and unknowable you can be certain
you feel both clear and unknowable you can see the bottom you can know no rocks are
hiding you know this slip is safe to return to every time this ship this little boat will stay
afloat keep this water spray across your body keep this wind chopping at your face this ship
that is your body will keep sailing across this water will accept the weight of you

Being Away from the Lake

that thing about a tree
and a forest and falling
no one to hear

but isn't there always at least one
body one eye one ear
to witness I was far away

in a cloud forest a tree did fall
it thundered down heavy
with rain and the howler monkeys

did what they are named to do
wasn't it Eve who named
every creature

alouatta, alouatta palliata
I don't know my Bible
stories I missed that boat

that heavy load that blesséd
water on my forehead
the lake is sacred

to some maybe even
to me when I am there
it renders me

a blue and borrowed thing the water the way
it slips through one's fingers even
if you press them tight

Distinctions

Mr. Yim could speak Washoe like a native,
                                        Melba says.
Story into story: voice like a willow thread.

Wašišiw means
                the people from here.

The lake is not a sea. You can see to the other shore.

A theory:
                our people could be said to have history.

18,000 years: a land bridge, ice, and ice,   and ice, a people
                                            walking.   Goodbye, family.

First the Yims owned a laundry,
                        then a gambling hall.
Sometimes our stories do match the conqueror's.

A theory:
                a separate entrance, not ice   but water.

13,500 years: boats on the wide,   wide sea.

A basket could be a kind of boat.   A carrying.

A theory:

        Maker of all Things
        counting seeds, the West Wind of mischief   blowing
        Wašišiw here.   Small, but rooted.

Mrs. Yim ran the bar, her name the same
                as my eldest auntie.
Mr. Yim played bouncer.

I like to drink martinis in the dark-paneled plush of the Big Four,
                names etched, glass
chilled just right in my hand.

Stanford, Huntington, Hollins, Crocker. I bet
              they'd been thrown
from more than one barstool.

A theory:

        stolen land, stolen jobs, Robber Barons.
        It's all one big family,   their pallor.

The Yims got in trouble   (with who? I forgot to ask,
             though I know exactly,   or inexactly)
when they allowed Washoe in, allowed them
           to eat off the dishware.

Melba lays out rank like silverware:
Second for Chinese,
Third for Indians. Somebody's always
the bigger brother.

A fallacy: Indians and Chinese
so much alike personally
that no human being could tell them apart

A degikup is shaped like a 應 量 器:
gift bowl : begging bowl
watertight : strainer
so many ways to hold sustenance

The glass is troublesome, breakable, grasped
in my ladylike hand.
My gun-hand, you know what I mean.
The weight.

A theory:
Wašiw might be part
of the Hokan family. Or:
it might be a language   isolate.

Charlie Crocker quit school and went off   alone
to support his family.

A theory:

        Cantonese is part of the Sino-Tibetan
        family, preserving more of Ancient Chinese
        than the other Chinese languages.

Chinese languages and dialects are
             isolating. Meaning:
one word to one sound, a singular   grammar.

A theory:

          to be human is to crave   the touch
                                  the company
        of others.

An isolate is a person or a thing that has been or become
                  isolated.

To be isolated is to be alone.

One man called him *a builder*, but he didn't lift   a single stone. Didn't hammer
                                                a single spike.

Pen to page   to checkbook   to legacy:
                              his son
commissioned the cathedral where I found   silence.
                     His mansion my school
                              of science and method.

Grace is one theory of salvation.

Another:

        the vast emptiness of space.

                              Light through stained glass

        enough to make me cry.

A theory

        is only a theory, though when I watched the dancers
        at the 'Itdeh, before I met Melba, I could see
one kind of resemblance.

To be human is to crave.

I stopped the provisions on them . . . stopped the butchers
                    from butchering, and used such coercive measures.

Reed baskets bare, yokes resting;

                rocks replaced shoulders.
How much do we know

          our way around hunger?

Forced to feed   forced to eat   from dishpans   they built
a separate entrance.

To be isolated

        is to be away

               from one's people.

They built an entrance, Melba says again, *just for us.*

The Ghost Ship

It's not that we didn't know. Your name, after all,
was the Ghost Ship, some kind of omen for what you'd become.

Ferrying somebody's sister, somebody's body, some bodies
across that fiery water: *elsewhere*. I don't believe

in elsewhere, an eternity of fire or sun. You were mannequin arms
and a rug on a dance floor. Some kind of baroque, you

were built of pallets and tar paper, old couches and terrycloth.
Everything that burns. You were art: always worth burning.

I don't believe in fate. I believe in grief, what it does to us.
Somewhere, somebody said: *intergenerational trauma*.

This isn't my grief, not mine to carry, a chalky
fire-crisped piano, the twanging sound of each string popped

by heat. Everything can be a performance. The hand-
lebars of a '65 Panhead. Your dark mustache

and aviator shades. You didn't die in this fire's crush:
a dream filled with opulence and hope.

Rents so high twenty-two people live and build
where they build beauty, too. This was and wasn't how we lost you—

timbers crashed in char and singe; staircase crumbled
in smoky crush—

The things we love to blame, the things we love
what ends us. One fire or another, inheritance

of doors burned shut. I think of you with no escape
I think of you   how could I not

        my first ghost   I wish I could
                sail back to you   I wish I could remember

Song for Great-Great-Grandfather

You, the first son: thus could you inherit.
   Thus could you be overthrown.
Your blinded baby the first son: thus could he

Be blinded. Thus could he become
   A teacher. Thus could he grow too old
For war. Thus could his first son die.

The war left nothing to inherit.
   Your grandchildren a scatter of seeds.
Thus could your first granddaughter root.

Thus did she build an empire from nothing,
   Did marry a third son, did bear ten children,
Did leave something to inherit:

To each of them, both sons *and* daughters—
   The rules turn: gradual as the engine's track.
A mountain must be accommodated.

But still, your first great-grandson: he receives
   The most. That biggest portion.
I am the only daughter.

Thus the track buckles
   Beneath my golden weight.
I have no sons, no daughters.

Thus I eat coal and gold and burn
   And burn and burn. My inheritance.

Lake of the Sky

The lake is a mirror, the sky's glittering edge.
Every perfect snowcapped mountain, each tree: doubled.

The endlessness of space, blue uniformity
rippling against its own boundaries, a color

beyond my word-finding skills burns into my mind's
eye: ferocious cyanotype. Name, metaphor:

another failed translation. Cloud-spread invention
of a white-banked imagination. I have learned

and forgotten why the sky is blue a thousand
times. I refuse to remember. To learn from our

mistakes. The sky knows itself by its reflection.
The lake contains us: constant companion, faithful

beyond any failure this earth might offer up.

Acknowledgments

Many thanks to the editors of the following publications, in which poems from this manuscript first appeared (some in slightly different forms):

Anomaly: the "Cold Shock" series
Bridges: "Dream of the Lake" and "Naming"; *CALYX*, "水客" and "Mercy"
Eastwind Ezine: excerpts of "高祖父 : A Correspondence : 太爺"
Indiana Review: excerpts of "高祖父 : A Correspondence : 太爺"
JuxtaProse Literary Magazine: "Song for Great-Grandfather"
Meridians: feminism, race, transnationalism: "Catalog of Writings Left by Chinese Railroad Laborers of the C.P.R.R."
Nimrod International Journal: "Burials," "Certainty," "Mythology," and "Tragedy"
Pinwheel: "遺產"
Poetry Northwest: "S---- Valley"
Prairie Schooner: "Property"
Queer Rain: "長衫"
Spoon River Review: "Failed Translations" and "Song for Great-Great-Grandfather"
The VIDA Review: the "Guest:" translation series
West Trade Review: "With a surface area of 191.6 square miles . . . ;"
wildness: "Intelligible."

Eighteen of the poems in this manuscript also appeared in the chapbook *Dream of the Lake* (Bull City Press, 2022).

Bountiful love and gratitude:

Rabble Collective (Somayeh Shams, Adrienne G. Perry, and Francine Conley), for your ongoing sisterhood, intellectual camaraderie, and critical friendship. Nathan McClain, Jennifer Funk, and Michael Jarmer, for invaluable feedback, close readership, and generosity.

Eleanor Wilner, for mentorship spanning nearly half my life. Rick Barot, Tommye Blount, Rachel Brownson, Gaby Calvocoressi, Daisy Fried, Camellia Grass, Rage Hezekiah, Susan Kiyo Ito, Kimberly Kruge, Ananda Lima, Martha Rhodes, Clare Ramsaran, Jennifer Sperry Steinorth, Noah Stetzer, L. Lamar Wilson, Nick White, Ross White, everyone who was part of the BIPOC Writing Party while it lasted, and surely a bunch of people I've forgotten to list. Every poet whose work kept me reading and writing and trying.

Gordon Chang, for lunch, sources, inspiration, and the beautiful artifact that is *Ghosts of Gold Mountain: The Epic Story of the Chinese Who Built the Transcontinental Railroad*. In my life, your timing was perfect. Eddie Wong, for being an early believer in these poems and for giving me the first public venue to share them with an audience.

My parents, Susan McDonough and Warren Mar; my wife, Sandy Metivier; Tioundra Body, Melissa Millan and Kelsey Green, Krissa Lagos and Julia Markish, Emma Olson and Tara Gonzalez, Alma Landeta and Kit Robbins, Steven Noble, Victoria Carter, Cal Calamia and Ariel Robbins, Stephanie Khaziran and Travis Westly, Nicole Rosendale and Bachul Koul, and the entire extended Mar family for support, questions, cheerleading, meals, space, and love along the way.

My ancestors, remembered and forgotten, haunting and at rest, better and worse than I have imagined you. 多謝晒。

The Washoe Tribe of Nevada and California, Indigenous people of the Lake Tahoe basin, for your perseverance and protection of your ancestral lands. Special gratitude for your collaboration, guidance, and patience to the Washoe Cultural Resources Advisory Council: Jo Ann Nevers, Dorothy McCloud, Lana Hicks, Floyd Wade, and especially Melba Rakow for sharing some of your stories and memories with me. Darrel Cruz for collaboration and connecting me with folks, and Herman Fillmore for additional help with orthography and translation.

The Chinese Railroad Workers Descendants Association (CRWDA) for planning and hosting the 2019 Golden Spike Conference in Salt Lake City, and to all the historians, filmmakers, and authors who shared their knowledge there.

The faculty and staff of the Chinese Immersion Program at West Portal Elementary from 1989–95. The language and history you taught me may not have survived intact, but you gave me the tools to imagine my way back.

Anita Har for your time and generosity in translating my broken Cantonese, and Kaylok Poon, my former student, for asking your mom to help me.

The Vermont Studio Center, Ragdale Foundation, and Storyknife for residencies where these poems were begun, worked on, and formed into a manuscript. All my co-residents for your art, community, and inspiration along the way.

The Wisconsin Poetry Series at the University of Wisconsin Press, edited by Sean Bishop and Jesse Lee Kercheval, for giving this book a home and a shape.

I turned to the following authors and artists for historical context, research, and stories, some of which may not be referenced directly in the Notes:

Gordon Chang, *Ghosts of Gold Mountain: The Epic Story of the Chinese Who Built the Transcontinental Railroad*

Stanford University, Chinese Railroad Workers in North America Project, https://west .stanford.edu/researchhistory-arts-and-culture/chinese-railroad-workers-north-america -project

Tim Greyhavens, The No Place Project, www.noplaceproject.com

Him Mark Lai, Genny Lim, and Judy Yung, eds., *Island: Poetry and History of Chinese Immigrants on Angel Island, 1910–1940*

Scott Lankford, *Tahoe Beneath the Surface*

Ursula K. LeGuin, "A Non-Euclidean View of California as a Cold Place to Be"

Michael Makley, *A Short History of Lake Tahoe*

Jo Ann Nevers, *Wa She Shu: A Washo Tribal History*

Jean Pfaelzer, *Driven Out: The Forgotten War Against Chinese Americans*

Rebecca Solnit, *Savage Dreams: A Journey into the Landscape Wars of the American West*

Sarah Winnemucca Hopkins, *Life Among the Piutes: Their Wrongs and Claims*

Ann M. Wolfe, ed., *Tahoe: A Visual History*

Notes

"Failed Translations": The original poem this sequence "translates" was carved on the wall of Angel Island by an unknown author. It is number 8 in the anthology *Island: Poetry and History of Chinese Immigrants on Angel Island, 1910–1940*, edited by Him Mark Lai, Genny Lim, and Judy Yung, where it can be found in both the original Chinese and the English translation.

"Dream of the Lake": The italicized text is an old sailor's saying.

"Stage 1: Cold Shock / Threat No. 1 Loss of Breathing Control" and "Threat No. 2 Heart and Blood Pressure Problems": The italicized text in both poems is from the National Center for Cold Water Safety's web page on cold shock. The titles of both poems, as well as the other Cold Shock poems, are also from this website: https://www.coldwatersafety .org/ColdShock.

"Portraits of the Ancestor": The poem responds to a variety of photographs in *Tahoe: A Visual History*.

"1870 census; Truckee, CA: Ah John, male, 18; occupation: prostitute": The inspiration for this poem comes from the one record of a male Chinese sex worker during railroad times. Maybe it was a typo by the census worker, but then again, maybe it wasn't. "The passion of the cut sleeve" is an old Chinese story about a queer emperor and his lover. The italicized text is from a white journalist's description of seeing as least one perceptibly queer (to him) railroad worker, who was additionally described as having his queue "braided with silk, and so elongated and increased in size that it completely threw his brethren in the shade. He might have vied with almost any lady of fashion in the perfection of his black hair." These quotes and the information about Ah John's census entry come from Gordon H. Chang's *Ghosts of Gold Mountain: The Epic Story of the Chinese Who Built the Transcontinental Railroad*.

"Stage 4: Circum-rescue Collapse": The original text was taken from the online article "4 Phases of Cold Water Immersion," Beyond Cold Water Bootcamp, http://www.beyondcold waterbootcamp.com/4-phases-of-cold-water-immersion#Circum-rescue%20Collapse, accessed in Fall 2016. The original site is no longer accessible but is quoted here: https://www.manitobafishingforum.com/threads/4-phases-of-cold-water-immersion.102641/.

"Fire Control": The "Truckee Method" was, as described in the poem, a plan of boycotting and essentially starving out the Chinese residents of Truckee in 1886. Charles McGlashan founded the Truckee Anti-Chinese Boycotting Committee, and he used the method's "success" as a "nonviolent" method (though the town's Chinatown was burned down more than once) to pursue a political career in California. The Committee published a document in 1885 stating, "We recognize the Chinese as an unmitigated curse to the Pacific Coast and a direct threat to the bread and butter of the working class." The other italicized term, "coolie slave," was commonly used to describe Chinese laborers in California, though they were neither coolies (indentured servants) nor slaves.

"高祖父 : A Correspondence : 太爺": "The mountains are calling . . ." is a quote from John Muir. "When you raise a daughter . . ." is something I misremembered being attributed as a common Chinese saying by Pearl S. Buck in *The Good Earth*. During early exposure to white folks, Chinese people commonly called white people barbarians and were disgusted by their public displays of affection.

"Tie": the italicized text (including misspelling) was written by Mark Hopkins in a private letter to fellow robber baron/railroad owner Collis P. Huntington as he described the conditions of laborers working in the bright, blinding snows. I read the excerpt in Gordon H. Chang's *Ghosts of Gold Mountain: The Epic Story of the Chinese who Built the Transcontinental Railroad.*

"Property": the quote from Lum May can be found in his statement from June 3, 1886, in the Washington State Historical Society archives, https://www.washingtonhistory.org/wp-content/uploads/2020/04/lumMayStatement.pdf, and at "The No Place Project: Chinese Voices," https://www.noplaceproject.com/chinese-voices.

"John Chinaman" and "Celestials": Both of these titles come from terms used to describe Chinese people in the United States during the mid to late 1800s. The former was more overtly offensive (similar in usage to another racialized nickname of the period, "Sambo,") while the latter was perceived as complimentary—or at least not pejorative—and derived from a translation of one of the names of the Chinese empire.

"Distinctions": Melba Rakow is an elder of the Washoe Tribe of Nevada and California, and a member of the Washoe Cultural Resources Advisory Council. The 'Itdeh is an annual gathering hosted by the Washoe Tribe on the shores of South Lake Tahoe. The two italicized quotes in the poem not ascribed to Melba are the words of Charles Crocker. The first ("so much alike personally . . .") described not a similarity between the two ethnic groups, but among them. Crocker and the CPRR did not pay Native American or Chinese laborers as individuals (as they did for white workers); instead, they hired them in crews of fifty to one hundred and paid all wages to a "headman" who could then pay out his brethren, since apparently it was too difficult for whites (who I am forced to assume Crocker means by "human being") to bother noticing that any people of color had faces, names, or other distinctive characteristics. I've taken the quote out of context for this poem, of course. His second quote ("I stopped the provisions . . .") describes Crocker's claim that his strategies finally broke the Chinese workers' strike of 1867, though this doesn't seem to align with historical facts. For more on the strike and its outcomes, see Gordon H. Chang's *Ghosts of Gold Mountain.*

"*The Ghost Ship*": The Ghost Ship was a live/work artists' collective built into a warehouse in Oakland, California. It caught fire during a party on December 2, 2016. Thirty-six people died of smoke inhalation, making it Oakland's deadliest-ever fire. The italicized line "a dream filled with opulence and hope" is an excerpt of a Facebook post by Ghost Ship founder and master tenant Derick Ion Almena, posted one day after the fire. Walter Mar died in a house fire in 1983.

"Lake of the Sky": This name/term is a mistranslation of a mispronunciation. The Wašiw word for Lake Tahoe is dáʔaw (pronounced Da ow), meaning simply "the lake." The Washoe people also refer frequently to dewʔá:gaʔa (pronounced Da ow a ga), meaning "edge of the lake." See Jo Ann Nevers's *Wa She Shu: A Washo Tribal History.* Somewhere the story got started that dewʔá:gaʔa meant "lake of the sky," which is in fact just white nonsense.

CAROLINE M. MAR is the great-granddaughter of a railroad laborer and the author of *Water Guest*, the Editors' Selection for the 2024 Wisconsin Poetry Series. She is also the author of *Special Education* (Texas Review Press), which won the 2019 X. J. Kennedy Prize, and the chapbook *Dream of the Lake* (Bull City Press). Carrie is a graduate of the MFA Program for Writers at Warren Wilson College, a member of Rabble Collective, and serves on the board of Friends of Writers. She is a longtime ninth-grade health educator in her hometown of San Francisco, and lives in Oakland, CA. She has been granted residencies at Storyknife, Ragdale, and Hedgebrook, among others. You can find her online at carolinemar.com.

WISCONSIN POETRY SERIES

Sean Bishop and Jesse Lee Kercheval, *series editors*
Ronald Wallace, *founding series editor*

How the End First Showed (B) • D. M. Aderibigbe

New Jersey (B) • Betsy Andrews

Salt (B) • Renée Ashley

(At) Wrist (B) • Tacey M. Atsitty

Horizon Note (B) • Robin Behn

What Sex Is Death? (T) • Dario Bellezza, selected and translated by Peter Covino

About Crows (FP) • Craig Blais

Mrs. Dumpty (FP) • Chana Bloch

Rich Wife (4L) • Emily Bludworth de Barrios

Shopping, or The End of Time (FP) • Emily Bludworth de Barrios

The Declarable Future (4L) • Jennifer Boyden

The Mouths of Grazing Things (B) • Jennifer Boyden

Help Is on the Way (4L) • John Brehm

No Day at the Beach • John Brehm

Sea of Faith (B) • John Brehm

Reunion (FP) • Fleda Brown

Brief Landing on the Earth's Surface (B) • Juanita Brunk

Ejo: Poems, Rwanda, 1991–1994 (FP) • Derick Burleson

Grace Engine • Joshua Burton

The Roof of the Whale Poems (T) • Juan Calzadilla, translated by Katherine M. Hedeen
and Olivia Lott

Jagged with Love (B) • Susanna Childress

Salvage • Hedgie Choi

Almost Nothing to Be Scared Of (4L) • David Clewell

(B) = Winner of the Brittingham Prize in Poetry
(FP) = Winner of the Felix Pollak Prize in Poetry
(4L) = Winner of the Four Lakes Prize in Poetry
(T) = Winner of the Wisconsin Prize for Poetry in Translation

Partially Excited States (FP) • Charles Hood

Ripe (FP) • Roy Jacobstein

Last Seen (FP) • Jacqueline Jones LaMon

Perigee (B) • Diane Kerr

American Parables (B) • Daniel Khalastchi

The Story of Your Obstinate Survival • Daniel Khalastchi

Saving the Young Men of Vienna (B) • David Kirby

Conditions of the Wounded • Anna Leigh Knowles

Ganbatte (FP) • Sarah Kortemeier

Falling Brick Kills Local Man (FP) • Mark Kraushaar

The End of Everything and Everything That Comes after That (4L) • Nick Lantz

The Lightning That Strikes the Neighbors' House (FP) • Nick Lantz

You, Beast (B) • Nick Lantz

The Explosive Expert's Wife • Shara Lessley

The Unbeliever (B) • Lisa Lewis

Radium Girl • Celeste Lipkes

Water Guest • Caroline M. Mar

Slow Joy (B) • Stephanie Marlis

Cowboy Park (FP) • Eduardo Martínez-Leyva

Acts of Contortion (B) • Anna George Meek

Blood Aria • Christopher Nelson

Come Clean (FP) • Joshua Nguyen

Bardo (B) • Suzanne Paola

Meditations on Rising and Falling (B) • Philip Pardi

Old and New Testaments (B) • Lynn Powell

Season of the Second Thought (FP) • Lynn Powell

A Path between Houses (B) • Greg Rappleye

The Book of Hulga (FP) • Rita Mae Reese

Surveille (B) • Caitlin Roach

Why Can't It Be Tenderness (FP) • Michelle Brittan Rosado